SPOT 50
Sharks

Camilla de la Bedoyere

Miles
KeLLy

First published in 2015 by Miles Kelly Publishing Ltd
Harding's Barn, Bardfield End Green, Thaxted, Essex, CM6 3PX, UK

Copyright © Miles Kelly Publishing Ltd 2015

2 4 6 8 10 9 7 5 3 1

Publishing Director Belinda Gallagher

Creative Director Jo Cowan

Editor Amy Johnson

Designer Rob Hale

Image Manager Liberty Newton

Production Manager Elizabeth Collins

Reprographics Stephan Davis, Jennifer Cozens, Thom Allaway

ISBN 978-1-78209-854-6

Printed in China

British Library Cataloguing-in-Publication Data
A catalogue record for this book is available from the British Library

ACKNOWLEDGEMENTS
The publishers would like to thank Mike Saunders for the artwork he has contributed
to this book. All other artworks are from the Miles Kelly Artwork Bank.

The publishers would like to thank the following sources for the use of their photographs:
Dreamstime.com 43 Naluphoto; 51 Marco Lijoi **FLPA** 7 Gerard Soury/Biosphoto; 52 Pete Oxford/Minden
Pictures **iStockphoto.com** 44 stephaniki2 **Naturepl.com** 9 Ian Coleman (WAC);
21 Ian Coleman (WAC); 25 Doug Perrine; 32 Ian Coleman (WAC) **Photoshot.com** front cover Oceans
Image; 49 NHPA **SeaPics.com** 31 Masa Ushioda **Shutterstock.com** 4(b) ilolab; 36 cbpix; 37 Sergey
Dubrov; 38 Ian Scott; 39 orlandin; 41 Ian Scott; 42 Rich Carey; 45 FAUP; 50 Rich Carey
Science Photo Library 34 Andy Murch/Visuals Unlimited, Inc.

Every effort has been made to acknowledge the source and copyright holder of each picture.
Miles Kelly Publishing apologizes for any unintentional errors or omissions.

Made with paper from a sustainable forest

www.mileskelly.net
info@mileskelly.net

CONTENTS

Tick the circles when you have spotted the species.

WHAT IS A SHARK?

Sharks are fish that live in oceans and seas. Many types of shark are predators, which means they hunt other animals to eat. Sharks have skeletons made of a substance called cartilage, which is softer than bone. Some sharks lay eggs but many give birth to their young, which are called pups. The pups are able to swim and hunt as soon as they are born.

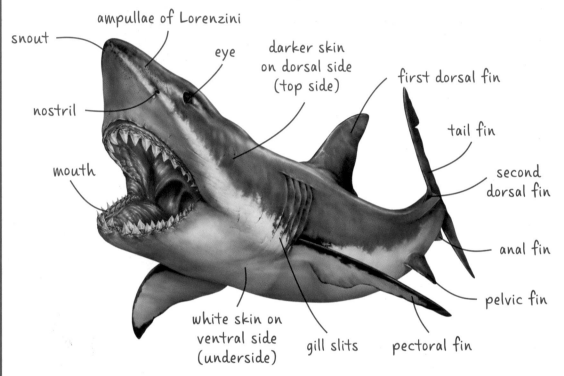

snout

ampullae of Lorenzini

eye

darker skin on dorsal side (top side)

first dorsal fin

tail fin

second dorsal fin

nostril

anal fin

mouth

pelvic fin

white skin on ventral side (underside)

gill slits

pectoral fin

WHERE IN THE WORLD?

Sharks are found in waters around the world. They are almost all marine fish, which means they live in salty seas, although some species do inhabit fresh water. Sharks are most common around coasts. Many species live in warm waters, but a few live in cold water around the Arctic. Sharks are rarely found in the Southern Ocean around Antarctica. The green areas on this map show the parts of the oceans where sharks are most common.

ARCTIC OCEAN

ATLANTIC OCEAN

PACIFIC OCEAN

PACIFIC OCEAN

INDIAN OCEAN

SOUTHERN OCEAN

SHARK ORDERS

There are about 400 species of shark, which scientists divide into eight large groups, called orders, and then into about 30 smaller groups, or families. This helps scientists to study and identify them. Shark orders and families have long scientific names, written in Latin. For example, goblin sharks belong to the Mitsukurinidae family, in the Lamniformes order.

Each species also has its own scientific name made up of two parts, so it can be easily identified across the world. The scientific name for the goblin shark is *Mitsukurina owstoni*. Scientists can identify which order a shark belongs to by looking at features such as its body shape, markings, behaviour and DNA.

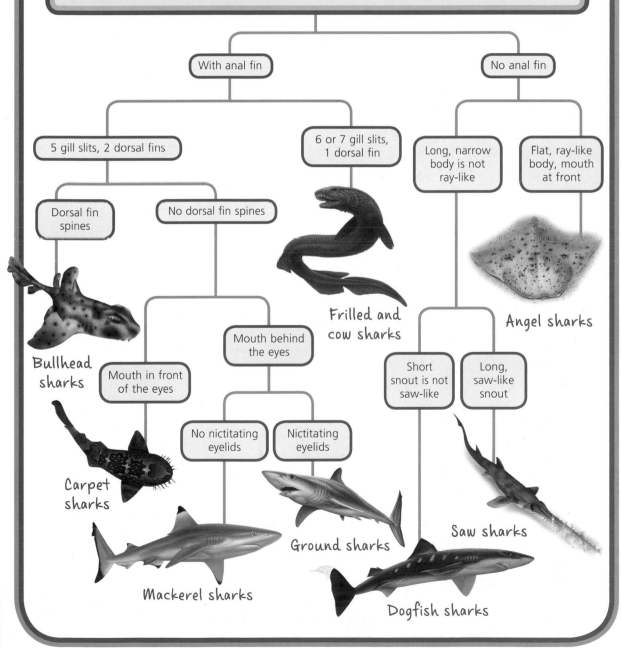

With anal fin

No anal fin

5 gill slits, 2 dorsal fins

6 or 7 gill slits, 1 dorsal fin

Long, narrow body is not ray-like

Flat, ray-like body, mouth at front

Dorsal fin spines

No dorsal fin spines

Bullhead sharks

Mouth in front of the eyes

Mouth behind the eyes

Frilled and cow sharks

Angel sharks

Short snout is not saw-like

Long, saw-like snout

Carpet sharks

No nictitating eyelids

Nictitating eyelids

Ground sharks

Saw sharks

Mackerel sharks

Dogfish sharks

ANGEL SHARK

Squatiniformes is the name of a large group of sharks called angel sharks, or monkfish. This angel shark is typical of the group, with a broad, flat body, a short snout and large fins. It has good camouflage and can hide on the seabed during the day. It is a strong swimmer and ambushes bottom-living fish, such as skates, as well as molluscs and crustaceans. The angel shark has been heavily fished, and recently its numbers have fallen dramatically.

SCALE

FACT FILE

Scientific name *Squatina squatina*

Size 1.3–1.8 m

Reproduction Between 7 and 25 pups are born in a litter

Habitat Mud or sands, inshore on coasts and in estuaries

Where in the world Northeast Atlantic around Europe and the top of Africa

Thanks to a flat, broad body it is easy for an angel shark to hide from prey by burying itself in sand on the seabed.

large, stocky body with very rough skin

grey, reddish or brown body with small white spots and black dots

flattened body

nasal barbels with a straight tip

PACIFIC ANGEL SHARK

The reddish-brown, patterned skin of a Pacific angel shark helps it blend into a rocky seabed. Its eyes are on the top of its head, allowing it to watch approaching prey while still hidden. Like many other sharks that live on the seabed, angel sharks mostly hunt at night when they are less likely to be attacked by bigger sharks. Numbers of Pacific angel sharks are low because they are caught for food.

SCALE

Pacific angel sharks use their shovel-shaped heads to partly bury themselves in shingle (small stones), hiding them from prey.

FACT FILE

Scientific name *Squatina californica*

Size Up to 1.5 m

Reproduction Up to 10 pups are born in a litter

Habitat Often around rocks or seaweed on the continental shelf

Where in the world Coasts of North and South America

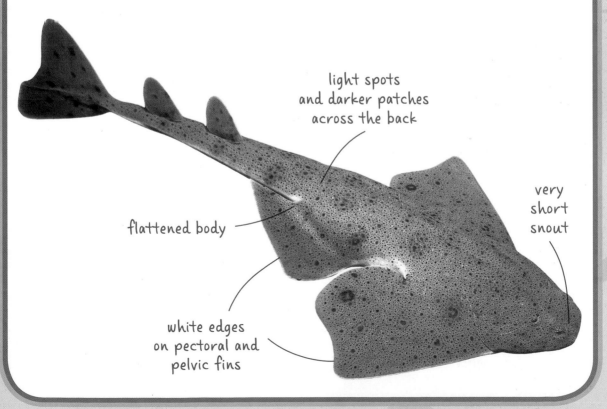

light spots and darker patches across the back

very short snout

flattened body

white edges on pectoral and pelvic fins

LONGNOSE SAW SHARK

Peculiar-looking creatures, saw sharks were common in the world's oceans millions of years ago, but are now found less frequently due to over-fishing. They have stocky bodies and very long slender snouts that are armed with rows of saw-like teeth. The snout is extremely sensitive to vibration and electrical fields, and is probably used to detect prey. Saw sharks gather in groups to feed and they mostly hunt small fish and crustaceans.

SCALE

FACT FILE

Scientific name *Pristiophorus cirratus*

Size 90 cm–1.4 m

Reproduction Up to 19 pups are born in the winter

Habitat Continental shelf and slope, on sandy or gravel seabeds

Where in the world Coastal waters and bays around southern Australia

The saw shark's soft barbels are like whiskers. They are very sensitive to touch and are used to find prey.

stocky body

long snout makes up a third of the body length

skin is yellow, brown or grey with some dark blotches, spots and bars

white underneath

long barbels

SPINY DOGFISH

This dogfish has a huge range and lives in coastal areas in many parts of the world. Spiny dogfish are slow swimmers and they migrate long distances to reach cooler waters in the summer. They are known to feed in very large groups, and the females also come together to give birth to their pups in nurseries in shallow waters. The spiny dogfish is also known as the piked dogfish, Pacific dogfish, spurdog and greyfish.

SCALE

FACT FILE

Scientific name *Squalus acanthias*

Size 90 cm–1.5 m

Reproduction About 6–8 pups are born in each litter

Habitat Coastal and inshore waters

Where in the world Across all oceans

These small sharks usually swim near the seabed, especially near the coast. They feed on fish and invertebrates.

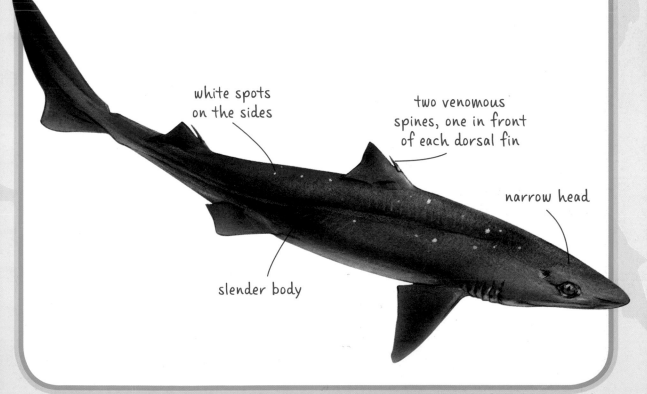

white spots on the sides

two venomous spines, one in front of each dorsal fin

narrow head

slender body

COOKIE-CUTTER SHARK

Abizarre way of feeding has given rise to this shark's common name of cookie-cutter, although it is also known as the cigar shark because of its body shape. Cookie-cutters live in deep waters and have light-making organs that attract other animals. When its prey approaches, the cookie-cutter lurches forward and bites it, using its sucking lips to grip. It then swivels around in a circle until it has removed a large chunk of flesh, the shape of a cookie.

SCALE

FACT FILE

Scientific name *Isistius brasiliensis*

Size 31–50 cm

Reproduction About 6 or 7 pups are born in a litter

Habitat Usually deep, tropical water near islands

Where in the world Atlantic, southern Indian and Pacific Ocean

These sharks spend the day lurking in deep water, but they swim upwards under cover of night when it is time to hunt.

small, cigar-shaped body

dark collar behind the head

short, bulbous snout

luminous (light-making) organs cover the skin on the lower surface

large, triangular and saw-like lower teeth and sucking lips

GREENLAND SHARK

This massive shark can grow as big as a great white, but it is considered harmless to humans. Greenland sharks are slow swimmers that hunt fish and large animals such as seals. It is thought they can put on bursts of speed to catch fast-swimming fish such as salmon. They also feed on carrion (the remains of dead animals). Many Greenland sharks are affected by a parasite that causes blindness.

SCALE

Small parasites called copepods attach themselves to a Greenland shark's eyes. Over time, the copepods can damage the eyes enough to blind the shark.

FACT FILE

Scientific name *Somniosus microcephalus*

Size 2.4–7.3 m

Reproduction It is thought that about 10 pups are born in a litter

Habitat Cold, deep water

Where in the world The cold waters of the North Atlantic and Arctic Ocean

broad tail used for bursts of speed

very large in size and heavy-bodied

short, rounded snout

dark or pale patches along the sides

PYGMY SHARK

Small and dark in colour, pygmy sharks are hard to observe and little is known about how they live. They have strong jaws with spear-like teeth and prey on deep-water squid, fish and some crustaceans. At night, pygmy sharks come close to the ocean surface, where food is plentiful. During the day they migrate down to deep waters or the seabed.

SCALE

This is one of the smallest sharks in the world. Pygmy shark pups are just 6 cm long when they are born.

FACT FILE

Scientific name *Euprotomicrus bispinatus*

Size 17–27 cm

Reproduction About 8 pups are born in a litter

Habitat Deep temperate waters by day, closer to the surface at night

Where in the world South Atlantic, South Pacific and Indian Ocean

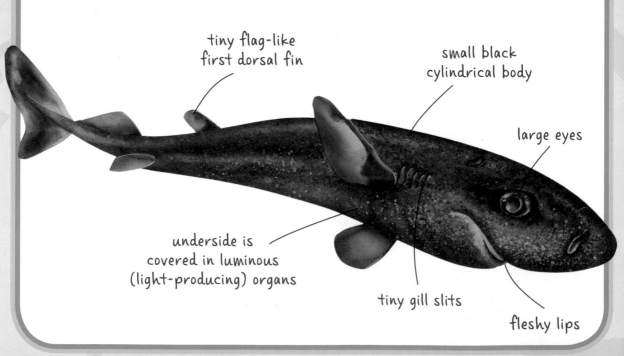

tiny flag-like first dorsal fin

small black cylindrical body

large eyes

underside is covered in luminous (light-producing) organs

tiny gill slits

fleshy lips

FRILLED SHARK

Considered rare, frilled sharks can live in a range of habitats and in all the world's oceans. They usually swim in deep water, where they prey on deep-water squid, although they do sometimes come to the ocean's surface, even at shallow coasts. Frilled sharks have large, frilly gill slits and their many teeth also look frilled, arranged in sets of five, with slender, spiked points.

SCALE

Each of the frilled shark's teeth has three sharp points. They are a good size and shape for gripping on to slippery squid.

FACT FILE

Scientific name
Chlamydoselachus anguineus

Size 92 cm–2 m

Reproduction 6–12 pups are born in a litter

Habitat Coastal and open ocean, to depths of up to 1500 m

Where in the world Found in areas of all oceans

flattened head

very short snout

six pairs of large, curved gill slits

teeth have sharp, spiked points

brown, black or grey-black skin

long, eel-shaped body

BLUNTNOSE SIXGILL SHARK

Sharks in the group Hexanchidae (cow sharks) have six or seven pairs of gill slits, and are mostly widespread in open oceans and coastal areas. Bluntnose sixgill sharks are most often found near the seabed, the continental shelf or slope, and deep-ocean features such as sea mounts. Skilled hunters, they feed on a variety of animals such as crabs, bony fish, rays, seals and even other sharks.

SCALE

FACT FILE

Scientific name *Hexanchus griseus*

Size 3–5.5 m

Reproduction Up to 108 pups are born in a litter

Habitat Found in most marine habitats

Where in the world Worldwide except in cold polar waters

Bluntnose sixgill sharks can be aggressive if they are provoked. They do not like to be touched by humans.

large, powerful body

broad head

large eyes

light-coloured stripe along the sides

six gill slits on each side

comb-shaped lower teeth

HORN SHARK

These sharks are named after the high ridges above their eyes, which give the appearance of horns. They use their muscular fins like limbs to clamber around the seabed, and are not good swimmers. Horn sharks are usually solitary, and hide in crevices and cracks where their mottled skin provides good camouflage. They are more active at night, when they hunt molluscs and crustaceans.

SCALE

Horn sharks have two dorsal fins, and each one has a sharp spine. The spines help protect the sharks from predators.

FACT FILE

Scientific name *Heterodontus francisci*

Size 58 cm–1.2 m

Reproduction 2 eggs are laid under rocks and in crevices every 11–14 days, for four months

Habitat Warm, shallow waters where there are caves and rocky crevices

Where in the world East Pacific Ocean from California to Peru

mildly poisonous spine in front of each dorsal fin

short, blunt head with high ridges above the eyes

small body

covered in small dark spots

broad, muscular paired fins used as limbs for clambering along the seabed

PORT JACKSON SHARK

Distinctive markings make Port Jackson sharks easy to recognize. Unlike most species of sharks, they lay eggs rather than giving birth to live young. They often breed close to shores and reefs, and the females gather to lay their eggs in the same places each year, in August and September. The eggs are wedged into rock crevices to keep them safe for up to a year before they hatch.

SCALE

It is thought that these sharks have good memories and can remember the best places to hide from predators.

FACT FILE

Scientific name *Heterodontus portusjacksoni*

Size 70 cm–1.7 m

Reproduction 10–16 eggs are laid every 8–17 days in the breeding season

Habitat Rocky seabeds in temperate coastal waters

Where in the world Off the coast of southern Australia

one spine in front of each dorsal fin

dark band between and below the eyes

black tail stripe

harness-shaped markings on the back

very small mouth

WHALE SHARK

This is the largest shark – and the largest fish – in the world. Whale sharks feed on plankton, krill and small fish, which they suck into their enormous mouths and gulp down. To feed, they swim slowly through warm waters near the ocean's surface, with their mouths open, and often hang vertically in the water. Whale sharks make massive migrations, travelling thousands of kilometres to reach the best feeding areas.

SCALE

FACT FILE

Scientific name *Rhincodon typus*

Size 6–21 m

Reproduction Up to 300 pups may be born in a litter

Habitat Various warm water habitats from the open ocean to shallow coasts and coral reefs

Where in the world Very wide distribution across warm and tropical waters, except the Mediterranean Sea

Inside a whale shark's mouth are rakers (plate-like sieves). They trap the food, while the water flows out of the gills.

large tail

massive body

chequerboard pattern of yellow or white spots across the back

broad, flat head with a short snout

huge, wide mouth

ZEBRA SHARK

Young zebra sharks have white stripes and spots on their bodies, and it is these markings that give the sharks their name. Zebra sharks usually hunt alone, and are most active at night. They chase their prey at speed, following it into crevices and cracks in rocky coral. Females lay large eggs, which are protected in leathery cases and anchored to the seabed with tufts of hair-like fibres.

SCALE

FACT FILE

Scientific name *Stegostoma fasciatum*

Size 1.5–2.5 m

Reproduction They lay eggs, although the quantity is unknown

Habitat Warm, coastal and shallow areas, especially around coral reefs

Where in the world Indo-west Pacific Ocean

Zebra shark pups can be easily distinguished from adults by their different skin pattern. They are about 30 cm long when they hatch.

the first dorsal fin is bigger than the second

ridges run along the dorsal surface and along the sides

large, flexible and slender body

large pectoral fins

rounded snout with short barbels underneath

TASSELLED WOBBEGONG

Animals that hide on the seabed often have patterned skin to help them blend in. They may also have extra growths that blur their silhouettes. Tasselled wobbegongs are good examples of both methods of camouflage. The lobes of skin, or 'tassels' that grow around their jaws look like seaweed and help to fool the sharks' prey of lobsters, crabs and other creatures that live on the seabed.

SCALE

A camouflaged wobbegong is almost invisible. It rests during the day and hunts at night, ambushing its prey with the help of quick reflexes.

FACT FILE

Scientific name *Eucrossorhinus dasypogon*

Size 1.2–1.3 m

Reproduction Unknown, but they probably give birth to live young

Habitat Shallow waters around coral reefs

Where in the world Southwest Pacific Ocean

broad, flattened body

nasal barbels appear 'tasselled'

dark blotches and lines on paler skin

'tassels' from the tip of the snout to the base of the pectoral fins

SPOTTED WOBBEGONG

Mostly nocturnal, spotted wobbegongs spend the day hiding in sandy places or dark crevices and caves. They use their superb camouflage to approach prey without being detected, and then lunge forwards in a rapid ambush. Spotted wobbegongs have wide, powerful mouths and can suck in their prey with the use of protruding jaws and an expanding throat. Wobbegongs may bite humans if they are disturbed.

SCALE

FACT FILE

Scientific name *Orectolobus maculatus*

Size 60 cm–3.2 m

Reproduction Up to 37 pups are born in a litter

Habitat Shallow water with hiding places, such as rocky or sandy shores and coral reefs

Where in the world Western Pacific Ocean, especially around Australia

Spotted wobbegongs can deliver a very painful bite. They have powerful jaws, and rows of sharp teeth.

yellow, green and brown markings

flattened body and head

pale spots, lines and blotches

long barbels are 'tasselled' and look like seaweed

NURSE SHARK

These sharks live in shallow coastal waters near people and often come into contact with them. They have been fished for food, oil and for their skins, which make a tough leather. Nurse sharks are not especially aggressive, but will bite hard if they are disturbed. They often rest in groups during the day, and at night hunt for bottom-living creatures by swimming close to the seabed.

SCALE

Nurse sharks lurk in small, dark places, particularly in the daytime. They have flexbile bodies and broad, smooth heads with barbels.

FACT FILE

Scientific name
Ginglymostoma cirratum

Size 2–3 m

Reproduction 20–30 pups are born in a litter

Habitat Shallow rocky waters or coral reefs, mangrove swamps and warm coastal shelves

Where in the world Tropical waters in the Atlantic and eastern Pacific Ocean

both dorsal fins are rounded

large first dorsal fin

long, slender tail

dark grey-brown skin

small teeth but very strong jaws

EPAULETTE CARPET SHARK

In general, carpet sharks – such as epaulettes – are small sharks that live in shallow, warm waters. Epaulettes lay their eggs in protective egg cases. The pups hatch from the eggs after about 120 days and feed on small marine animals such as worms, shrimps and young fish. Epaulettes are most active at dusk and at night, and they are able to swim, clamber and crawl through shallow water.

SCALE

FACT FILE

Scientific name *Hemiscyllium ocellatum*

Size 60 cm–1.1 m

Reproduction Up to 50 eggs are laid at a time

Habitat Shallow water coral reefs and tidepools

Where in the world Western Pacific Ocean, around New Guinea and northern Australia

Epaulette carpet sharks have large, strong pectoral fins. They use them like limbs to move along a rocky seabed.

dark spots across the body except on the snout

extremely long tail

large black spot with a white margin, behind each pectoral fin

creamy-brown skin

small, slender body

GREAT WHITE SHARK

Also known as pointers, great whites are the world's best-known and most-feared sharks. They are supreme hunters that combine strength and speed to catch prey. Great whites can survive in a large range of ocean habitats because they are able to maintain a constant body temperature, even in cold waters. They often come close to shore in search of seals, large fish and even dolphins.

SCALE

FACT FILE

Scientific name *Carcharodon carcharias*

Size 3.5–6 m

Reproduction Between 2 and 10 pups are born in a litter

Habitat All waters but common inshore and around rocky reefs

Where in the world Worldwide throughout most oceans

Great white sharks are fast, powerful swimmers. They are strong enough to leap out of the water.

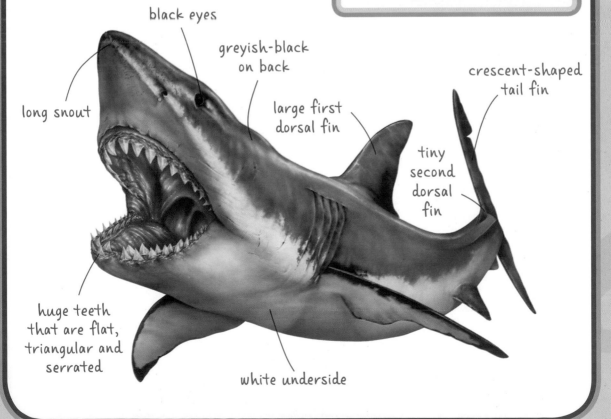

black eyes

greyish-black on back

crescent-shaped tail fin

long snout

large first dorsal fin

tiny second dorsal fin

huge teeth that are flat, triangular and serrated

white underside

SHORTFIN MAKO

Mackerel sharks are a group **that is known for speed and superb hunting skills.** The shortfin mako is probably the fastest of all sharks, and is able to travel great distances in a short time. Shortfin makos prey on other fish including marlins and swordfish, which are also extremely fast swimmers. They can make large leaps out of the water, and have even been known to jump onto boats when hooked on fishing lines.

A mako is not only fast, it can undertake long-distance swims. One shark swam 2130 km in just 37 days.

SCALE

FACT FILE

Scientific name *Isurus oxyrinchus*

Size 2–4 m

Reproduction Between 4 and 30 pups are born in a litter

Habitat Most habitats, including warm oceanic and coastal waters

Where in the world Worldwide in all tropical and temperate waters

long, pointed snout

large, black eyes

back is a metallic blue or purple

streamlined body

large, blade-like hooked teeth — visible even when mouth is closed

white underside

crescent-shaped tail fin

PORBEAGLE SHARK

Although they are stouter and rounder than other mackerel sharks, porbeagles are still able to pursue their prey at great speed. They are rarely seen in the winter months, when they spend more time offshore, in deep water. In the summer, porbeagles move inshore to feed where they are more vulnerable to being caught for food and oil. Porbeagles often come close to divers and fishing boats, but they are not dangerous to humans.

SCALE

FACT FILE

Scientific name *Lamna nasus*

Size 1.5–3 m

Reproduction 4 pups are normally born in a litter

Habitat Cool waters, generally inshore but also in the open ocean

Where in the world North Atlantic Ocean and across cooler waters in the Southern Hemisphere

A porbeagle's body temperature is warmer than the surrounding water. This helps it to swim fast.

white smudge on the back edge of the first dorsal fin

stout, heavy body

sharply pointed snout

large gill slits

BASKING SHARK

These are the second largest sharks in the ocean (after whale sharks). Basking sharks feed near the surface of the water, cruising slowly with their mouths open to swallow small marine animals (plankton). They often feed in large groups, following the plankton as it moves with the ocean currents. Little is known about basking sharks and how they reproduce, although it is thought they give birth to live young, rather than lay eggs.

SCALE

Water gushes into a basking shark's mouth and flows out of its body through the gill slits, trapping the plankton.

FACT FILE

Scientific name *Cetorhinus maximus*

Size 5–10 m

Reproduction They give birth to live young

Habitat Found near coasts and in open ocean, near the surface

Where in the world Worldwide in temperate seas and oceans

pointed, conical snout

very large in size

crescent-shaped tail

huge gill slits that almost encircle the head

huge mouth with tiny teeth

GOBLIN SHARK

Mysterious and unique, goblin sharks are placed in their own group within the mackerel sharks. Few examples have been found, so little is known about their lifestyle. Goblin sharks swim in very deep waters where there is no light, and may be able to use their long snouts to detect electric signals given off by prey. Their jaws can extend forwards, out of their mouths, to grab small fish and squid.

SCALE

FACT FILE

Scientific name *Mitsukurina owstoni*

Size 2.6–5 m

Reproduction Unknown

Habitat Deep waters

Where in the world The Atlantic, western Indian and Pacific Ocean

A goblin shark's snout is long and flat. There are 26 teeth on the top jaw and 24 on the lower jaw.

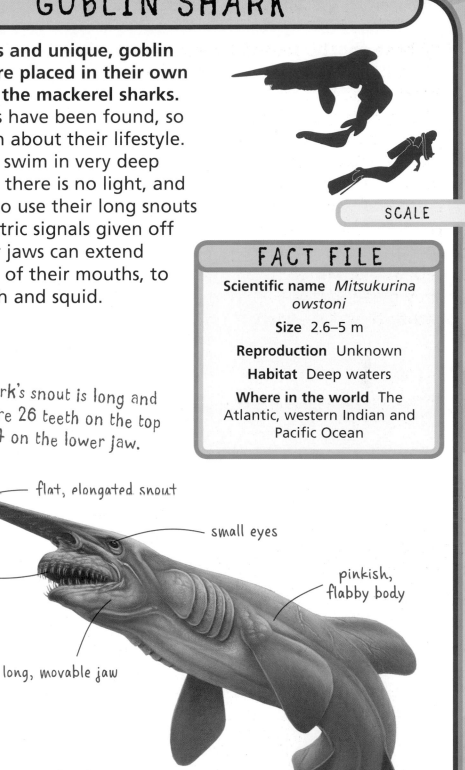

flat, elongated snout

small eyes

long, slender teeth

pinkish, flabby body

long, movable jaw

long tail fin

THRESHER SHARK

These sharks are named after their unusual method of hunting – they swipe their long, muscular tails at prey to stun or wound it. It is thought that thresher sharks may even work together to herd schools of fish into an area before attacking. They also sometimes use their tails to strike and stun seabirds. These sharks can be found close to land, especially when it is time for the females to give birth.

SCALE

Few sharks can breach (jump out of the water) at all, but threshers can make huge leaps clear of the water.

FACT FILE

Scientific name *Alopias vulpinus*

Size 2.5–6 m

Reproduction Between 2 and 6 pups are born in a litter

Habitat Coasts and open oceans

Where in the world Worldwide distribution in cool to temperate waters

very long upper tail lobe

tiny second dorsal fin

fairly large eyes on the side of the head

narrow, pointed pectoral fins

small head with a short snout

MEGAMOUTH SHARK

Little is known about megamouth sharks because very few have ever been found. It is thought they spend the day in deep waters, but rise to the surface at night to feed. They may have light-producing organs in their mouths that attract prey. Megamouths are highly sensitive to noise and movement, and descend quickly when they are disturbed.

SCALE

FACT FILE

Scientific name *Megachasma pelagios*

Size 4–5.5 m

Reproduction Unknown

Habitat Open ocean and coastal waters

Where in the world Warm and tropical waters worldwide

The megamouth shark was first discovered in 1976, in Hawaii. They are not thought to be dangerous to humans.

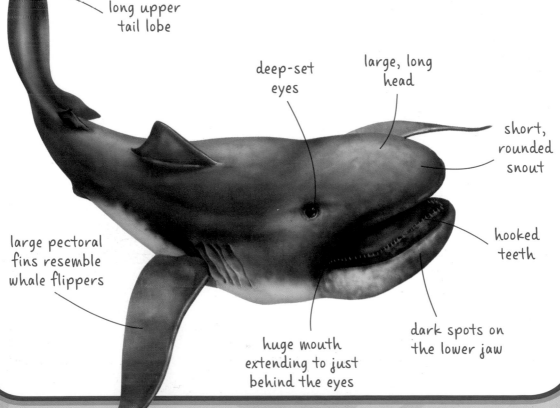

long upper tail lobe

deep-set eyes

large, long head

short, rounded snout

hooked teeth

large pectoral fins resemble whale flippers

dark spots on the lower jaw

huge mouth extending to just behind the eyes

SANDTIGER SHARK

These large sharks are also known as spotted raggedtooths or grey nurse sharks. They can be identified by their clusters of long, slender and extremely sharp teeth. Sandtigers often gather in large groups to feed and they may sometimes migrate to cooler waters in the summer. The developing pups eat unfertilized eggs and other growing pups while still inside their mother, which is why only two survive to be born.

Sharks with lots of long slender teeth — like the sandtiger shark — usually hunt small, slippery fish such as mackerel.

SCALE

FACT FILE

Scientific name *Carcharias taurus*

Size 2.2–4.3 m

Reproduction 2 pups are born in a litter

Habitat Coastal waters around caves, gullies and reefs

Where in the world Warm and tropical seas, especially the Atlantic and Indo-west Pacific Ocean, and the Mediterranean Sea

long tail fin

light brown with a paler underside

large, heavy body

long gill openings

long mouth extends behind the eyes

BONNETHEAD SHARK

These small hammerhead sharks have a very distinctive head shape that is rounded between the eyes. Bonnetheads are most active during the day and hunt blue crabs, small fish, shrimp and shellfish near the seabed. They have superb senses and are able to detect the smallest movements made by animals nearby. Bonnetheads are hunted by other sharks, and by humans for food.

SCALE

FACT FILE

Scientific name *Sphyrna tiburo*

Size 50 cm–1.5 m

Reproduction Between 4 and 16 pups are born in a litter

Habitat Around coasts, usually up to 80 m deep

Where in the world Tropical seas around the Americas

Bonnethead sharks cruise close to the seabed. If they do not keep swimming they sink to the bottom.

tall dorsal fin

upper tail lobe is almost straight

flat, rounded head

small, slender body

mouth is on the underside of the head

SCALLOPED HAMMERHEAD

Able to live in a range of habitats, scalloped hammerheads can be found from the open ocean to inshore estuaries and bays. They are mainly found in shallow waters, but older sharks can swim to depths of 1000 metres. Scalloped hammerheads gather in groups to feed. Their main prey are bony fishes, rays, squid and octopuses. Although these sharks were once common, they have been heavily fished.

SCALE

Hammerheads have big appetites. Up to 50 stingray spines have been found in just one hammerhead's mouth and guts!

FACT FILE

Scientific name *Sphyrna lewini*

Size 1.4–4.2 m

Reproduction Around 13–30 pups are born in a litter

Habitat Continental shelves to depths of 380 m

Where in the world Worldwide in warm and tropical waters

arched head, in the shape of a hammer

light grey or bronze with a white underside

long upper tail lobe

indentations on the front of the head give a scalloped appearance

pectoral fins may be slightly darker

GREAT HAMMERHEAD

These sharks are similar in appearance and size to scalloped hammerheads, and have a similar range. However, their heads are straighter along the front edge, and their skin is dark grey. They mostly live in warm seas near continental shelves, but in the summer they may move towards cooler waters. Their teeth are large, triangular and serrated. Great hammerheads are powerful hunters and feed on bony fish, stingrays and other sharks.

This shark's wide head may help it to find prey using its electro-senses. It also helps the shark to change direction quickly.

FACT FILE

Scientific name *Sphyrna mokarran*

Size 2.2–6.1 m

Reproduction Between 6 and 40 pups are born in a litter

Habitat Far offshore as well as shallow coastal areas and coral reefs

Where in the world Worldwide in tropical waters

large, hammer-shaped head

first dorsal fin very tall and curved

slightly humped back

much larger upper tail lobe than lower

LEOPARD SHARK

Named after their distinctive markings, leopard sharks prefer warm to cool water and are often seen close to the shore, or in estuaries and bays. They swim in groups that may include other small sharks such as smooth-hounds and dogfish. Their patterned skin gives these sharks camouflage when swimming in cloudy waters such as seaweed beds. Leopard sharks mostly feed on small animals that live in mud on the seabed.

SCALE

A group of sharks is called a shoal or a school. Swimming in a group may help sharks, such as leopard sharks, stay safe from predators.

FACT FILE

Scientific name *Triakis semifasciata*

Size 70 cm–2 m

Reproduction Between 4 and 33 pups born in a litter

Habitat Sandy or muddy bays and estuaries

Where in the world Northeast Pacific Ocean, especially San Francisco Bay

pattern of dark saddle marks and spots

rounded first dorsal fin

broad, short snout

pectoral fins are large and triangular

GALAPAGOS SHARK

Preferring clear waters close to shores, Galapagos sharks can even be found at depths of just 2 metres. They can be aggressive towards people, but usually arch their backs as a warning before attacking. Galapagos sharks often gather in groups. They feed mostly on fish, squid and octopuses near the seabed, but they have been seen preying on much bigger animals, such as sea lions. Galapagos sharks are hunted by larger sharks.

SCALE

These sharks are inquisitive animals. They have been known to approach swimmers, divers and boats.

FACT FILE

Scientific name *Carcharhinus galapagensis*

Size Up to 3.7 m

Reproduction Between 6 and 16 pups are born in a litter

Habitat Around coasts, in clear water

Where in the world Worldwide around tropical islands

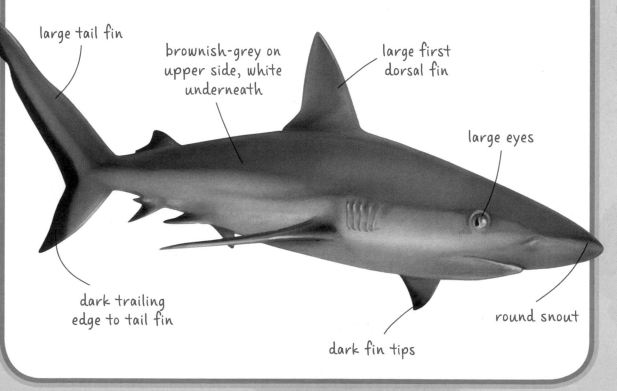

large tail fin

brownish-grey on upper side, white underneath

large first dorsal fin

large eyes

dark trailing edge to tail fin

round snout

dark fin tips

GREY REEF SHARK

These sharks are often seen in groups around coral islands, especially at night when they are most active. They are curious sharks that often swim close to divers, and near the water's surface. If they are threatened, grey reef sharks swim with their heads and tails swaying to warn other animals – or people – to move away. They hunt bony fish, squid, octopuses and shelled creatures.

SCALE

FACT FILE

Scientific name *Carcharhinus amblyrhynchos*

Size 1.1–2.3 m

Reproduction Between 1 and 6 pups are born in a litter

Habitat Near lagoons and coral islands in tropical and subtropical waters

Where in the world Pacific and Indian Ocean

During the day, groups of grey reef sharks gather in shallow waters, especially over areas where the seabed is flat.

large eyes

grey body with white underside

black or dusky tip on all fins, except the first dorsal

long snout

large, narrow pectoral fins

trailing edge of the tail fin has a wide black margin

SILKY SHARK

One of the most common species of sharks, silky sharks are often fished for food and for their skins. They are aggressive sharks that can be dangerous to humans, although they normally give warnings – they hunch their backs and raise their heads – before attacking. Silky sharks sometimes swim in shallow water although they are mostly found at depths of 200 metres or more. They prey on bony fish, squid, octopuses and crabs.

Some sharks, including silky sharks, can be made to go limp by turning them over. This technique allows scientists to handle them safely.

SCALE

FACT FILE

Scientific name *Carcharhinus falciformis*

Size 1.9–3.3 m

Reproduction Between 2 and 14 pups are born in a litter

Habitat Near continental shelves and in open ocean

Where in the world Worldwide in tropical seas

large, slim body

bronze to grey body with a white underside

dark tip to all fins except the first dorsal fin

large eyes

very smooth skin that appears almost metallic

long and narrow pectoral fins

small jaws

BULL SHARK

Most sharks need clear, salty ocean water to survive, but bull sharks are also able to live in fresh water such as rivers. They swim slowly until they attack their prey, when they chase it at speed. They pursue many types of animals, from seabirds and turtles to dolphins and fish, and even attack land mammals feeding at the water's edge. Bull sharks are dangerous for humans to encounter.

SCALE

Bull sharks are famous for not being fussy about what they eat — they even devour bull shark pups if they find them!

FACT FILE

Scientific name *Carcharhinus leucas*

Size 1.6–3.4 m

Reproduction Up to 13 pups are born in a litter

Habitat Lagoons, bays and channels between islands and river mouths

Where in the world Worldwide in tropical and subtropical seas

dusky fin tips

large, heavy body

broad head

very short, broad snout

large pectoral fins

small eyes

OCEANIC WHITETIP SHARK

Once common, numbers of oceanic whitetips have fallen sharply in recent times because they are caught for food and for their fins. These sharks prey on a range of animals including fish, squid, seabirds and shelled animals. Oceanic whitetips are aggressive and fight other sharks for food. They mostly live far offshore, but have been known to come inshore, and even attack humans.

SCALE

These sharks often swim with pods of pilot whales. No one knows why, but the whales may lead the sharks to swarms of squid.

FACT FILE

Scientific name *Carcharhinus longimanus*

Size 1.8–4 m

Reproduction Up to 15 pups are born in a litter

Habitat Usually far offshore in warm open ocean

Where in the world Worldwide in tropical and warm temperate waters

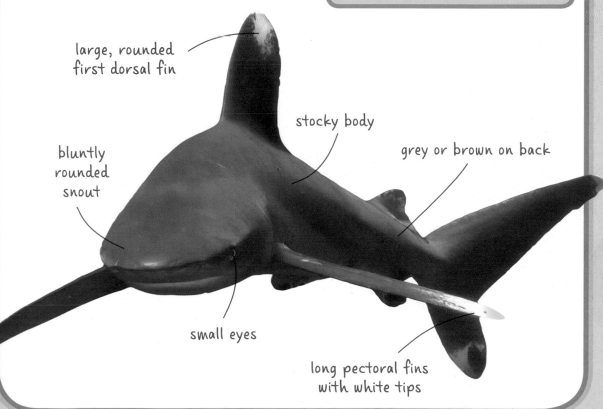

large, rounded first dorsal fin

stocky body

grey or brown on back

bluntly rounded snout

small eyes

long pectoral fins with white tips

BLACKTIP REEF SHARK

As their name suggests, the dark tips of these sharks' dorsal fins are a noticeable feature, especially when they swim in shallow seas and the fins poke above the water's surface. These common sharks are often found swimming in groups around coral reefs. They are powerful swimmers and often investigate divers, but rarely attack them. Blacktip reef sharks mostly feed on small, bony fish, squid, octopuses and crustaceans.

FACT FILE

Scientific name *Carcharhinus melanopterus*

Size 90 cm–1.9 m

Reproduction Between 2 and 4 pups are born in a litter

Habitat Very shallow water around coral reefs and reef flats

Where in the world West Pacific and Indian Ocean, and eastern Mediterranean Sea

Young blacktip reef sharks occupy the shallowest waters of a reef. Older sharks often swim deeper.

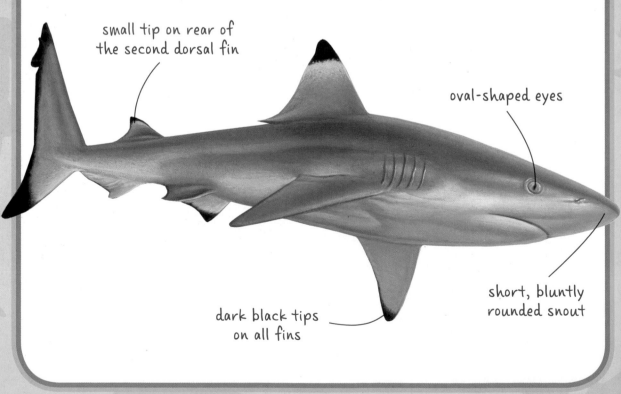

small tip on rear of the second dorsal fin

oval-shaped eyes

short, bluntly rounded snout

dark black tips on all fins

DUSKY SHARK

These sharks live in a wide range of locations. They go on long migrations to mate and give birth, or to reach cooler water in the summer and warmer water in the winter. Pups are born in shallow water, near the coast, and often stay in these nursery areas while they grow. Larger sharks often stay away from shallow water, so the dusky shark pups are less likely to be eaten there.

SCALE

FACT FILE

Scientific name *Carcharhinus obscurus*

Size 2.8–4 m

Reproduction Between 3 and 14 pups are born in a litter

Habitat Continental shelves to depths of 400 m

Where in the world Worldwide in tropical and warm waters

Dusky sharks are slow-growing fish. They do not have pups until they are about 20 years old and they live to 40 or more.

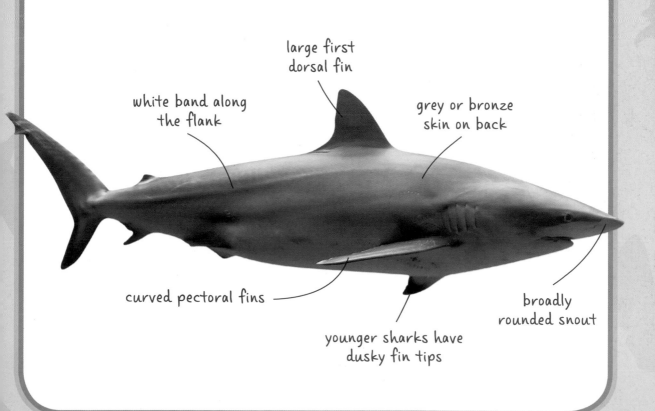

large first dorsal fin

white band along the flank

grey or bronze skin on back

curved pectoral fins

broadly rounded snout

younger sharks have dusky fin tips

CARIBBEAN REEF SHARK

These are the most common sharks seen in the Caribbean Sea, especially around coral reefs. They prefer shallow water, where they feed mostly on bony fish. The pups are about 70 centimetres long at birth and are preyed on by tiger sharks and bull sharks. Caribbean reef sharks are common around dive sites, but they rarely attack humans.

SCALE

FACT FILE

Scientific name *Carcharhinus perezi*

Size 1.5–2.9 m

Reproduction Between 3 and 6 pups are born in a litter

Habitat Coral reefs

Where in the world West Atlantic Ocean and Caribbean Sea

Some sharks, such as the Caribbean reef shark, have a special third eyelid called a nictitating membrane. This eyelid can move across the eye to protect it.

large, dark grey body

both dorsal fins have short tips

large circular eyes

tail fin may be dusky

white or yellowish underside

TIGER SHARK

The striped appearance of tiger sharks gives them their name, although these markings usually fade as a shark ages. These are big sharks that can, occasionally, grow to lengths of 7 metres or more. They are fast swimmers, and their speed and great size mean they need to eat more than most sharks. They will eat almost any animal they find.

Tiger sharks that live in coastal waters often mistake human rubbish for food, and swallow metal cans, plastic tubs and glass bottles.

FACT FILE

Scientific name *Galeocerdo cuvier*

Size 2.3–6.5 m

Reproduction Between 10 and 80 pups are born in a litter

Habitat Coastal areas and open ocean

Where in the world Worldwide in tropical and temperate seas

first dorsal fin much larger than the second

large head

grey back with black to dark grey bars and blotches

big mouth with large, sharp teeth

broad, bluntly rounded snout

LEMON SHARK

Named for their pale yellow-brown skin, lemon sharks are common, and live close to the coast in shallow waters. They even swim around river mouths and upstream for short distances. Lemon sharks usually swim alone, or in groups of up to 20 sharks. They are most active at night, when they hunt stingrays, small sharks and seabirds. These sharks lie on the seabed during the day.

SCALE

FACT FILE

Scientific name *Negaprion brevirostris*

Size 2.2–3.4 m

Reproduction About 13 pups are born in a litter

Habitat Shallow tropical waters including reefs, bays and mangrove swamps

Where in the world Western coast of the Americas, and east Atlantic and east Pacific Ocean

Young lemon sharks live amongst mangrove roots, where they can find food and stay safe from bigger sharks.

both dorsal fins are large and a similar size

wide, flat head

stocky body

short snout

yellow-brown skin

BLUE SHARK

These graceful sharks are known for their slender bodies and incredible migrations. They probably travel further and longer than any other shark, as they move between feeding and mating areas. Blue sharks occasionally come close to shore, but they mostly live in the open ocean and often travel in groups. They are curious about swimmers and boats, and can be dangerous to humans. Blue sharks circle their prey before attacking.

FACT FILE

Scientific name *Prionace glauca*

Size 1.8–3.8 m

Reproduction Between 15 and 30 pups are born in a litter

Habitat Open ocean, to depths of about 350 m

Where in the world Worldwide in temperate and tropical waters

A blue shark has an ideal body shape for swimming fast and for very long distances. Its long slender tail is packed with muscles.

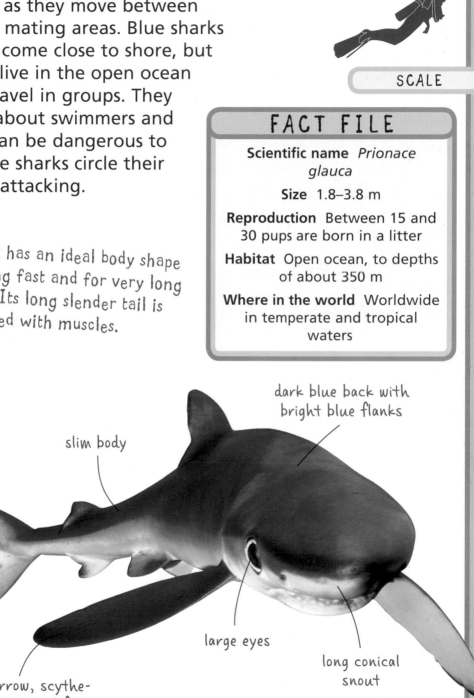

slim body

dark blue back with bright blue flanks

large eyes

long conical snout

long, narrow, scythe-shaped pectoral fins

WHITETIP REEF SHARK

These slender sharks are common in reef areas, although their numbers have fallen in recent years. They live in shallow water but usually stay close to the seabed, where they often rest in caves or crevices. Whitetip reef sharks are most active in the evening and at night, when they can find reef fish and crustaceans, such as crabs, to eat.

SCALE

Whitetip reef sharks often rest in large groups, piled on top of each other in caves. Each shark usually has a favourite place to rest.

FACT FILE

Scientific name *Triaenodon obesus*

Size 1–2 m

Reproduction Up to 5 pups are born in a litter

Habitat Shallow waters around coral reefs

Where in the world Wide-ranging across the Pacific Ocean

brilliant white tips on first dorsal and upper tail fin

grey-brown in colour

very short, broad snout

slender body

cleaner wrasse fish eat parasites and dead skin from the mouth and gills

oval-shaped eyes

BLACKTIP SHARK

Rarely swimming to depths of more than 30 metres, blacktip sharks are found around river mouths, and in estuaries, muddy bays and mangrove swamps. These are fast predators that chase schools of fish, occasionally leaping out of the water and spinning in the air. Blacktip sharks usually give birth to their pups in the late spring or summer. The pups stay where they were born until they are a few years old.

SCALE

FACT FILE

Scientific name *Carcharhinus limbatus*

Size 1.4–2.5 m

Reproduction Up to 10 pups are born in a litter

Habitat Coastal areas, in shallow water

Where in the world Widespread worldwide in tropical and subtropical areas

Blacktips can be aggressive and have been known to attack – but not kill – humans. They take a small bite then swim away.

white band across the flank

high first dorsal fin

grey back, white underside

long, narrow and pointed snout

most fins have black tips

long gill slits

small eyes

BRONZE WHALER

Also known as narrowtooth sharks and copper sharks, bronze whalers are common. They live in coastal areas to a depth of around 100 metres. Bronze whalers are often seen around river mouths, shallow bays and in estuaries, especially at times when females are giving birth. They mostly feed on squid, octopus and fish, and sometimes follow shoals of fish such as sardines.

SCALE

FACT FILE

Scientific name *Carcharhinus brachyurus*

Size 2–3 m

Reproduction Between 13 and 24 pups are born in a litter

Habitat Warm and temperate waters, mostly close to the shore

Where in the world Indo-Pacific and Atlantic Oceans, and Mediterranean Sea

Bronze whaler pups grow inside their mother's body for 12 months before they are born, when they measure about 65 cm long.

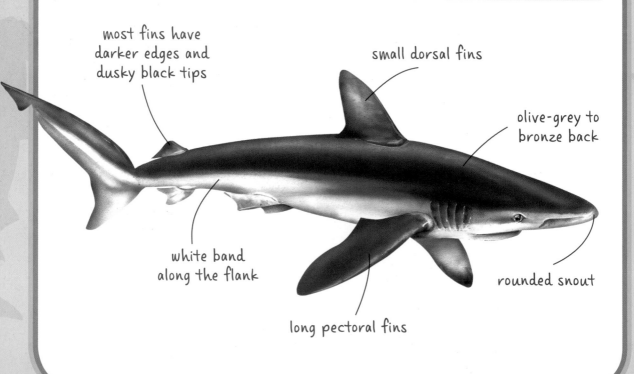

most fins have darker edges and dusky black tips

small dorsal fins

olive-grey to bronze back

white band along the flank

long pectoral fins

rounded snout

COMMON SKATE

Also known as blue or flapper skates, common skates used to live in large numbers in European coastal waters. They have been fished so heavily in recent times that they are now at risk of extinction. These large fish are long-living, and may reach 50 years of age. Common skates mostly feed on animals on the seabed, especially fish. Their long, slender tails carry a row of up to 18 thorny spines, which help to protect them from predators.

Skates swim gracefully above the seabed, flapping their enormous fins like wings in the water.

FACT FILE

Scientific name *Dipturus batis*

Size Up to 2.9 m long

Reproduction About 40 eggs are laid a year

Habitat Around coasts, usually up to 200 m deep

Where in the world Eastern Atlantic Ocean

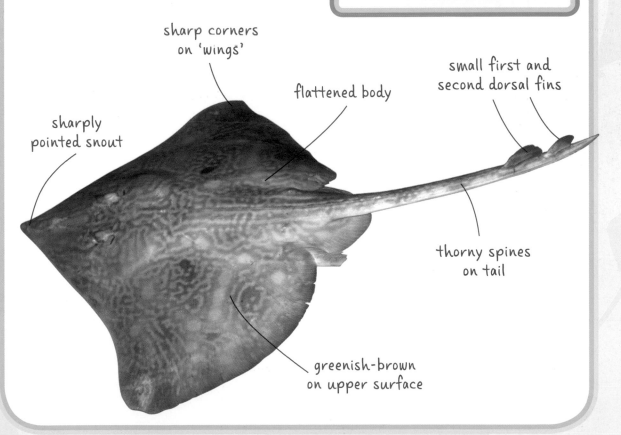

sharp corners on 'wings'

flattened body

small first and second dorsal fins

sharply pointed snout

thorny spines on tail

greenish-brown on upper surface

THORNBACK SKATE

As their name suggests, these skates have many prickly thorns on their backs and tails. The thorns swell and thicken at their bases when the fish mature, and are then called 'bucklers'. The mottled blotches on the skates' backs help them to blend into the sunlit shallows, where shadows are cast on the seabed. Thornback skates prey on crustaceans, such as shrimps and crabs, and fish.

SCALE

FACT FILE

Scientific name *Raja clavata*

Size Up to 1.2 m long

Reproduction Females lay up to 160 eggs a year

Habitat Usually found in shallow coastal waters

Where in the world Eastern Atlantic Ocean, Baltic Sea and parts of Indian Ocean

Females usually grow more thorns on their body as they get older, while males tend to lose thorns, especially on their pectoral fins, or 'wings'.

tail is as long as the body

disc-shaped body

body and tail are covered with thorns

body is pale but covered with dark blotches

GIANT MANTA RAY

These rays are remarkable in many ways. They are massive animals yet they can move gracefully through the water by gently flapping their 'wings'. Manta rays are able to leap out of the water, possibly to communicate with one another, and they have the largest brain of any fish. Despite their size, manta rays feed on tiny plankton. A newborn manta ray may be up to 1.5 metres from fin tip to fin tip.

SCALE

Manta rays can leap and somersault, and groups of rays sometimes take it in turns to jump out of the water this way.

FACT FILE

Scientific name *Manta birostris*

Size Up to 7 m wide

Reproduction One or two young are born at a time

Habitat From coasts to the open ocean

Where in the world Worldwide in warm waters of major oceans

large lobes help to guide food into the mouth

eyes are on the sides of the head

usually dark on the upper side

gills are on the underside of the body

huge pectoral fins form 'wings'

cream to white on the underside

COMMON STINGRAY

Well camouflaged and difficult to see on the seabed, common stingrays hunt for crustaceans such as crabs, as well as other shelled animals and fish to eat. They have many rows of grinding teeth, which can crush hard shells. Common stingrays are able to defend themselves from attack using a large venomous spine on a whip-like tail. The sting caused by the spine can cause pain and paralysis.

SCALE

Stingrays wriggle about when they settle on the seabed. Small stones and sand cover their backs, hiding them from their prey.

FACT FILE

Scientific name *Dasyatis pastinaca*

Size Up to 2.5 m long

Reproduction Up to 7 young are born at a time

Habitat Sandy shallow water to depths of 200 m

Where in the world Eastern Atlantic coasts and Mediterranean Sea

slender tail is longer than the body

upper side is a solid brown, grey or olive-green

no dorsal fins

front edges of the disc are almost perfectly straight

short snout

GULF TORPEDO

Also known as marbled electric rays, gulf torpedoes have beautiful markings that provide them with good camouflage on the seabed. They swim slowly by moving their tails, rather than their wing-like pectoral fins. When hunting, torpedoes lie on the seabed until prey animals come near. They then stun or kill their prey using an electric shock that is generated in organs on either side of the head, and guide it towards their mouth using their pectoral fins.

SCALE

Gulf torpedoes arch their backs to signal that they feel threatened and are about to produce an electric shock.

FACT FILE

Scientific name *Torpedo sinuspersici*

Size Up to 1.3 m wide

Reproduction Between 9 and 20 young are born at a time

Habitat Sandy shallow water to depths of 200 m

Where in the world Indian Ocean, Arabian Gulf and Red Sea

tiny eyes

flattened body

dark red or blackish-brown body with cream or gold markings

short, thick tail

wide pectoral fins connect head to body

SHOVELNOSE GUITARFISH

Guitarfish are named after their strange body shape, which is a mixture of shark and ray body shapes. Like many other members of the ray family, they prefer shallow water and hunt near the seabed. They feed on shelled animals, such as clams, and small fish. Shovelnose guitarfish normally live alone, but females may gather in big groups in the spring to give birth.

SCALE

These bizarre fish have more than 100 small, rounded teeth. Blunt teeth are perfect for crushing crabs and shellfish.

FACT FILE

Scientific name *Rhinobatos productus*

Size Up to 1.7 m long

Reproduction Up to 28 pups are born at a time

Habitat Shallow waters, near beaches, bays and estuaries

Where in the world Eastern central Pacific Ocean

row of thorny spines on back and tail

triangular body shape

long, pointed snout

thick, shark-like tail

olive-brown skin colour

SMALLTOOTH SAWFISH

Although their bodies are more shark-like in shape, sawfish belong to the ray family. They have a long snout with a toothed 'saw' that can be used to rake through sand, disturbing prey. The saw is also used to swipe and slash through shoals of fish. It is lined with up to 64 teeth, and there are also up to 12 rows of teeth in the fish's mouth. Smalltooth sawfish were once common around the world, but they are now close to extinction.

SCALE

Sawfish pups are born with their toothed saws in place, but the saws can bend so they don't damage the mother when the pups are born.

FACT FILE

Scientific name *Pristis pectinata*

Size About 5.5 m long

Reproduction Up to 20 pups are born at a time

Habitat Shallow salt water and fresh water

Where in the world Worldwide

upper side is covered with rough scales

underside is smooth and white

brown-blue skin

long saw is lined with teeth

GLOSSARY

Ampullae of Lorenzini Special sense organs around a shark's head that help it to find its prey. They detect the electricity made by another animal's muscles.

Barbels Long, fleshy growths on a shark's snout that are used to touch and feel the seabed, and find prey.

Breed To reproduce (when a shark makes eggs or pups).

Camouflage The way that patterns and colours on an animal's skin or coat help it to blend in with its surroundings.

Continental shelf The area of the seabed next to the land, where the water is shallow.

Continental slope The area where the continental shelf ends and the seabed slopes down to the deep ocean.

Crustacean A type of invertebrate with a shelled body such as a crab, lobster or shrimp.

Dorsal fin A fin on a fish's back. Most sharks have two dorsal fins, with the first being the largest.

Electro-sense A sense that allows sharks to detect electricity produced in another animal's body.

Estuary An area where a river (which has fresh water) meets the sea (which has salty water).

Extinction When a species of animal dies out forever.

Gills The breathing organs of a fish.

Habitat The place where an animal lives.

Invertebrate An animal that does not have a backbone, such as crustaceans and molluscs.

Krill A small, shrimp-like crustacean.

Litter When a shark has more than one pup at a time, the group of pups is called a litter.

Mangrove A type of tree or shrub that grows in coastal areas, especially around estuaries.

Migration A long journey that animals go on, usually to find food, mates or good places to breed.

Mollusc A type of invertebrate. Most molluscs live in the sea and can be soft-bodied, such as squid, or shelled, such as shellfish.

Nocturnal Animals that are more active at night than in the day.

Nursery The area where female sharks go to lay their eggs or give birth.

Parasite An animal that lives on or in another animal, causing it harm.

Pectoral fin The fin on a shark's side, nearest its head. Sharks have two pectoral fins, which are used to lift the shark as it swims and stop it from rolling over.

Plankton Tiny sea creatures and plants that drift along with the ocean currents.

Predator An animal that hunts other animals to eat.

Prey An animal that is hunted by predators.

Serrated Sharp and saw-like. Some sharks have teeth with serrated edges.

Snout The front of a shark's head that includes the nose and mouth.

Solitary An animal that lives alone, not in a group or family.

Temperate Places that do not experience extremes of temperature.

Tropical Places that lie around the Equator, between the Tropic of Cancer and the Tropic of Capricorn. They usually have hot, wet climates.